First published 2016 by Retro Inc Books
www.nickmackie.co.uk
© 2016 Nick Mackie

Updated 2019 due to Boris being crowned Prime Minister

The rights of Nick Mackie to be identified as the author and illustrator of this work have been asserted by him in accordance with the Copyright, Designs and Patents Act, 1988.

ISBN 978-09563290-73

BIRTH

Alexander Boris de Pfeffel Johnson was born on June 19, 1964.

New York, USA

Boris is a direct although illegitimate descendant of George II.
(George II is his Great x 8 Grandfather)

Regale Boris in the pageantry of his Royal ancestor.

Boris is a huge fan of Keith Richards.

He wanted to be the Rolling Stones guitarist in his youth.

Help Boris become a Rock 'n' Roll Legend.

Boris has a passion for playing Tennis and Whiff - Waff (Table tennis).

He once challenged former Wimbledon winner Boris Becker to a match.

Dress Boris as his hero Boris Becker.

SUPERHERO

Captain Britannia.

Will Boris Britannia save the nation?

Boris apparently loves singing the song 'Old man River'.

Boris as Old Father Thames.

Dick Whittington - The original Mayor of London.
If the PM job falls through there is always Panto.

Oh no there isn't!

The streets of London are paved with gold...

Boris is a keen cyclist and introduced the
Boris Bike to London.

HANGING AROUND

Boris famously got stuck on a zip wire in Victoria Park
during the London 2012 Olympic celebrations.

Help Boris relive that glorious moment.

THE BULLINGTON CLUB

Boris studied at Eton and Oxford.
He was also a member of the infamous Bullingdon Club.

Help Boris regain his youth and squeeze back into his costume.

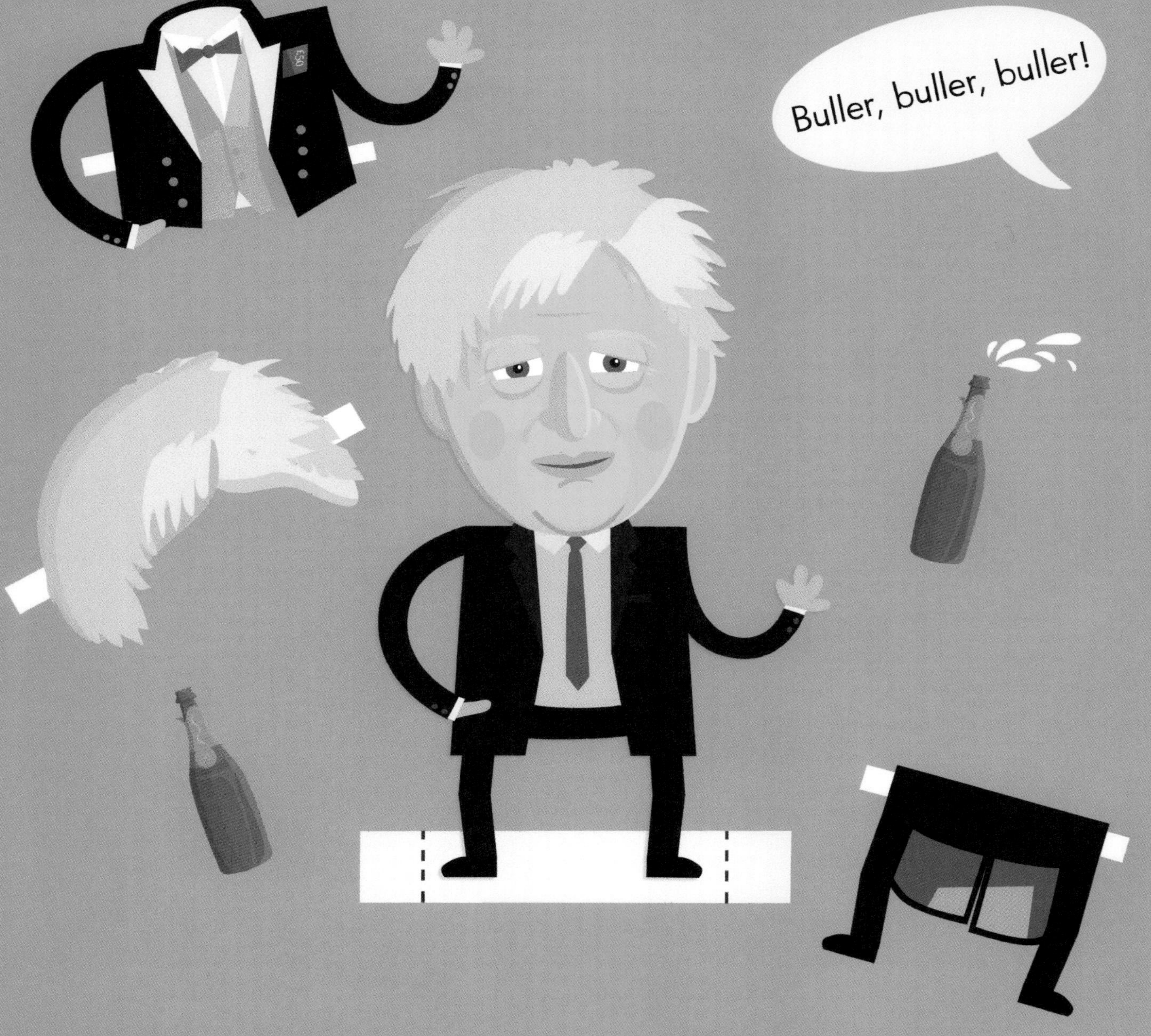
Buller, buller, buller!
£50

Boris Bond

Boris once compared himself to
James Bond.

(Daniel Craig jokingly suggested Boris might be cast as the next 007)

CARRY ON CAMPING

Boris has said he is a big fan of camping.

Help Boris recreate this classic British film
and find his inner 'Babs' or 'Sid'.

MR BRICK & MR KIPPER

'Brick, you will not be alone!'
Boris presented a house brick at the 2014
Conservative Party conference.

In 2019 Boris held up a kipper and blamed the EU for fictitious regulations.
Boris likes holding things up in the air.

A BETTER BLAH BLAH

Boris has rated his chances of becoming PM as 'slightly better than those of being decapitated by a frisbee, blinded by a champagne cork, locked in a disused fridge or reincarnated as an olive'.

On 23/07/19 Boris Johnson was crowned leader of the Conservative Party and thus Prime Minister of the UK.
About 160,000 Tory party members were able to vote.
The UK itself has about 46 Million eligible voters.

HOW TO

1: Stick the images onto card

2: Cut out

3: Assemble parts

(Glitter optional)

nickmackie.co.uk

Please contact me with any comments you may have.
It's great to hear from readers.
mackiebook@gmail.com

or tweet me at @nickmackiebook

Printed in Great Britain
by Amazon